AROUND
CHIPPING
NORTON
IN OLD PHOTOGRAPHS

AROUND
CHIPPING
NORTON
IN OLD PHOTOGRAPHS

COLLECTED BY
THE CHIPPING NORTON
LOCAL HISTORY SOCIETY

ALAN SUTTON
1987

Alan Sutton Publishing Limited
Brunswick Road · Gloucester

First published 1987

British Library Cataloguing in Publication Data

Around Chipping Norton in old photographs.
1. Chipping Norton (Oxfordshire)—History
—Pictorial works   2. Chipping Norton
(Oxfordshire)—Description—Views
I. Chipping Norton Local History Society
942.5'71   DA690.C545

ISBN 0-86299-457-8

Typesetting and origination by
Alan Sutton Publishing Limited.
Printed in Great Britain by
WBC Print Limited, Bristol.

CONTENTS

INTRODUCTION

Chipping Norton, standing as it does 650 feet above sea level on the edge of the Cotswolds, is a town of great antiquity. Although no authentic records exist before Domesday, the near presence of the Rollright Stones suggests the site is one which would commend itself to those who formerly chose the tops of hills to take up their dwellings. Roman coins have been found in the vicinity and a carved stone head believed to be of Roman origin was discovered at Glyme Farm.

The name is a corruption of the Saxon words 'ceapen' – to buy, and 'Neprune' – northern, therefore meaning Market of the Northmen.

Little is heard of events in Chipping Norton after Domesday, although a castle was erected there in the reign of King Stephen, some traces of which remain at the 'Castle Banks' on the north side of the church.

A Charter was granted by King John to the Lord of the Manor giving him leave to hold a fair at Chipping Norton for four days every year and the town formerly had the right to send two members to Parliament, until the inhabitants petitioned to be released from this privilege owing to the expense involved.

The Borough was incorporated on 27 February 1606 when it was governed by two Bailiffs and twelve Burgesses.

In the old coaching days Chipping Norton was the resting place for coaches running between Worcester and London and was well provided with inns for the victualling and accommodation of both man and beast during this flourishing period. Chapel House, half a mile to the east of the town, was a very popular posting house and was frequently used by Samuel Johnson and Boswell. It was here in 1776 that Dr Johnson delivered his famous panegyric on Taverns. 'There is no private house' he said 'in which people can enjoy themselves so well as a capital tavern . . . you are sure you are welcome, and the more noise you make, the more trouble you give, the more good things you call for, the welcomer you are'. Queen Victoria and her mother, the Duchess of Kent, slept there around the year 1886 when passing through the neighbourhood.

Many of the buildings shewn in the following photographs depict businesses which have now ceased. Hitchman's Brewery, established in 1796 and once the source of great activity and employment, is now only marked by a group of houses built on the site in Albion Street called Hitchman's Drive. Bliss's extensive Tweed Mill, rebuilt after a great fire in 1872, now stands empty. In the nineteenth century the Mill had a reputation for the quality of its tweed and the cordial relations between the owner and the workers. At its peak it employed 700 men and women. The gas works which formerly stood next to the Mill has been demolished. The closing of the railway line to passenger traffic in 1962 was followed within a few years by the taking up of the track. New industries have however been attracted to the town and in 1962 Parker Knoll set up a branch factory in London Road which now employs 400 workers.

The Town Hall in the centre of the town was built in 1842 and was designed by G.S. Repton. In order to make room for it the old elm tree, which had stood on the site for some 200 years and was unique in that it was a rookery, was felled, much to the consternation of the local populace.

The most beautiful piece of architecture in the town is the almshouses in Church Street founded by Henry Cornish in 1640 to accommodate eight poor widows. The impressive gateway bears the inscription 'Remember the Poor'.

The parish church, built in the Perpendicular style, is of great interest and beauty and is a reminder of the days when this part of England was the centre of a flourishing woollen industry. The hexagonal porch is one of only three in the country. The nave, with shafts going right through to the large and beautiful clerestory windows, is of special note. A fine collection of brasses taken up when the aisles were relaid is now displayed on the wall in the St John's Chapel.

In 1860 the Heythrop Hunt built its new kennels on the Worcester Road and the cry of the hounds is a familiar sound at feeding time. The pack is one of the foremost in the country and attracts many followers who come to live in the surrounding countryside. It has also provided many nostalgic photographs.

The photographs forming this book are taken from the collections of members of the Chipping Norton Local History Society.

SECTION ONE

The Town

THE MARKET PLACE showing the drinking fountain.

THE SALVATION ARMY BAND in the Market Place.

CARS IN THE MARKET PLACE *circa* 1920.

AN OLD VIEW OF CHIPPING NORTON showing the old elm tree and the Market Hall, 1747.

AN ETCHING OF THE MARKET PLACE showing the Town Hall and Miss Lydiatt's toy shop on the extreme right.

MARKET DAY in the town centre.

THE OLD RED LION INN being demolished to make a road through to Albion Street.

THE HOUSE WITH THE BAY WINDOW was formerly the Horse & Groom public house, closed in 1914, now demolished and used for the Guildhall car park.

A.A. WEBB'S SHOP in 1905.

A.A. WEBB'S SHOP being demolished in 1969 to widen New Street.

THE COTTAGES KNOWN AS BLACK BOY YARD which led from the High Street to Albion Street. Mr Cox is standing by the pump.

D.R. SIMMS, the jewellers shop on High Street, rebuilt in 1901 after the fire.

THE CHIPPING NORTON CO-OPERATIVE WHOLE-SALE SOCIETY premises in High Street.

A CO-OPERATIVE SOCIETY VAN in West Street.

MR & MRS SMITH'S SWEET SHOP in West Street, occupied later by their daughter, Mary Jane Lane.

EMPLOYEES OUTSIDE T.K. PETTIPHERS & SON'S grocers shop – now the Auto Spares shop.

INTERNATIONAL STORES – now the premises of Granny's Kitchen.

MR R.E. MINCHIN, Saddler and Harness maker outside his shop in the Market Square. The business was established in 1795. This now forms part of the Bunch of Grapes Inn.

A. GROVE & SON'S MEN outside the new Chipping Norton Post Office, opened 29 November 1931 including Harry Ryman and John Barlett of Little Compton.

BURFORD CORNER. The building behind the sign post is the old Liberal Club – demolished for road widening.

WALKER & ATKINSON the corn merchants adjoining the Fox Hotel – Mr Albert Guy is on the left-hand side.

MRS CAREY AND HER SON CECIL outside their shop in New Street.

BRINDLE'S SHOP in the High Street. These premises are now the offices of the Cheltenham & Gloucester Building Society.

THE MARKET SQUARE showing the water tank in the centre of the picture. This was built during the war as an emergency supply in case of fire.

THE DEMOLITION OF THE TANK in November 1955.

THE CASTLE BANKS on the north side of the church.

THE ALMSHOUSES in Church Street.

ONE OF THE NINE PILLARS FROM THE OLD MARKET HALL which was demolished in 1842 to make way for the Town Hall. This column now stands on the lower side of the Town Hall.

The Masonic Temple, Chipping Norton.

Photo, Eric Guy

THE MASONIC LODGE in Over Norton Road built in 1898.

THE NATIONAL CHILDREN'S HOME in New Street.

A SISTER AND CHILDREN from the National Children's Home going for a drive.

HILL LODGE, now the Chipping Norton War Memorial Hospital.

MEMBERS OF THE RED CROSS ASSOCIATION. Back row, left to right: Kitty Prentice, Nora Candy, Nancy Mott, Olive Harris, Florrie Lord, –?–, Mary Mann. Middle row: Edith Bick, Betty Cragg, Phyllis Claridge, Freda Yelf, Primrose Lord, –?–. Front row: Mrs Hutchinson, Miss Griffin, Mrs Daly, Mrs Allen.

THE OPENING OF THE WAR MEMORIAL HOSPITAL by Mrs Daly. The Mayor, Ernest Hall and Mr Toy on the right.

NURSING STAFF AND PATIENTS outside the hospital.

MR FRANK PACKER and his apprentice Jim Shadbolt in the workroom at his photography shop in High Street.

MR TOM HEATH with Mr Weston's butchers van.

BUILDING THE ODDFELLOWS HALL in London Road 1909.

THOMAS BURDEN AND STAFF outside the newly completed Oddfellows Hall.

WILLIAM BLISS was born in Chipping Norton in 1810 and took over the running of Bliss Mill in 1835.

THE REMAINS OF THE OLD MILL on the common after the fire in 1872.

THE PRESENT MILL which was built in 1872.

THE FORMER GASWORKS below the Mill.

MR HARRY BEALE at the Gasworks.

ROMAN HEAD found at Glyme Farm, now exhibited in the town museum.

LOCAL LADS fishing in the common brook 1923. Left to Right: Bert Reeves, Leslie Langton, Leslie Reeves, Cyril Hands, George Fiddes, Dennis H. Lewis, Donald Hall and Frank Hawtin.

RATS CAUGHT IN THE TOWN'S SEWERS. In the centre is Mr Bowen and on the right Mr Sinden (Town Clerk).

JIM SHADBOLT, aged two, in his best clothes.

Hotels and Public Houses

THE WHITE HART HOTEL before the arch was filled in.

THE CROWN & CUSHION HOTEL.

THE BLUE BOAR HOTEL in Goddard's Lane.

THE FOX HOTEL.

THREE ADJOINING PUBLIC HOUSES in New Street. The George, The Blue Lion and the King William – now all closed.

THE BUNCH OF GRAPES INN before alteration.

A GATHERING outside the Chequers Inn.

THE TAVERN OUTING TO WINDSOR RACES – 18 August 1934. Back row: Wilston Page, John Kay, Mr Witham, Bill Cattell, Dickie Worth, Alf Lewis, Charlie Simms, –?–, Dennis Lewis, Syd Cross, Ramsey Gibbs, Mr Canning, Fred Pick, Mr Baker, Mr Williams. Middle row: Sid Hewitt, –?–, Billy Aldridge, Mr Hannis. Front row: Roy Williams, Alf Fisher, Mr Radbone, Harry Watson, Bill Scarsbrook.

THE FOX & HOUNDS, Worcester Road.

THE QUIET WOMAN, Southcombe.

SECTION THREE

Churches

Chipping Norton.

ST MARY'S CHURCH.

THE INTERIOR OF ST MARY'S CHURCH.

THE HEXAGONAL SOUTH PORCH of St Mary's church.

REVD & MRS ARKLE with members of the Mothers Union, November 1934.

St. Mary the Virgin Church, Chipping Norton.

ST MARY'S CHURCH from the north side.

HOLY TRINITY CHURCH. CHIPPING NORTON.

HOLY TRINITY CHURCH, London Road. The bell tower has now been removed.

THE BAPTIST CHAPEL, New Street.

THE RAINBOW BAZAAR in the Baptist Schoolroom. Now the room is used as Chipping Norton Local History Museum.

MEMBERS OF THE SALVATION ARMY outside their Barracks in Spring Street. This is now the home of Chipping Norton Theatre.

THE PRIMITIVE METHODIST CHAPEL, now 20A and 20B Distons Lane.

THE MISSION HUT which formerly existed in Common Lane, Worcester Road. Services were conducted there on Sunday nights by officers of the Church Army centre.

THE METHODIST CHAPEL in West Street.

Occasions and Events

THE PROCESSION TO THE CHURCH on the occasion of King Edward VII's Coronation in 1901.

SETTING THE TABLES for the dinner to celebrate the Coronation, 1901.

QUEEN VICTORIA'S JUBILEE CELEBRATION in Chipping Norton 1887.

THE MAYOR, MR STANLEY WYKES, greeting HM the Queen on her visit to Chipping Norton during her tour of Oxfordshire.

Back row: Mrs Randle, Miss Knibbs. Front row: Mrs G. Somerton, Mrs Wright, Mrs Mealin, Mrs Shepherd, Mrs Pick, Mrs Burford, Mrs T. Gray, Nancy Marshall, Frank Shepherd.

CORONATION DAY, 1937.

THE MAYOR, MR JOHN GRANTHAM takes the first slice off the ox which was roasted to celebrate the Silver Jubilee of HM the Queen. June 1977.

CLUB DAY 1881. Members of the Old Elm Tree Lodge of Oddfellows. The Banner was borrowed from a Banbury Lodge as the Chipping Norton Lodge had not yet acquired their own. The Old Red Lion Inn, now demolished, is shown adjoining the Newmarket Inn.

JUNIOR MEMBERS OF THE SONS OF TEMPERANCE at the Hospital Saturday celebrations in 1911.

HOSPITAL SATURDAY 1919. Back row: Dorothy Robinson, Dorothy Weston. Front row: Daisy Hayman, Hilda Burbidge, Gladys Roberts, Vera Burden, Olive Simms, –?–.

MR & MRS HUBERT PACKER on the Merry-Go-Round at the Hospital Carnival 1921.

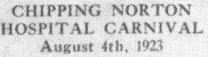

CHIPPING NORTON
HOSPITAL CARNIVAL
August 4th, 1923

"DAILY MIRROR"
JULY 23rd, 1923

14 WEEKS' DROUGHT AT ENGLAND'S DRIEST SPOT

Chipping Norton in Despair at Return of Heat Wave

Potatoes are no bigger than marbles, plants are withered and brown, while sorry-looking apples and pears lie scattered about the ground in orchards.

Despite a cooling breeze yesterday a temperature of 75degs. in the shade was registered. The river was crowded, and by afternoon hardly a boat was to be obtained.

Please OBSERVE the RIVER ☞ ☞

F. Packer, Chipping Norton Copyright
Everything in Photography

DENNIS LEWIS fishing with his companion, Leslie Langton.

MR JIM ROBINSON with his Austin Seven. Seated: Dorothy Weston and Dorothy Robinson.

HOSPITAL SATURDAY, 1934.

THE CROWNING OF THE CARNIVAL QUEEN, Miss Joyce Hern, by the Mayor, Mr Swann 1935.

CHIPPING NORTON FIRE ENGINE at Chipping Norton Hospital Carnival 1938. Horace Warmington, George Wright, Bill Stokes, Bill Wright, Ernie Morris. Standing: Chief Officer E. Simms, Third Officer R. Gibbs.

CHIPPING NORTON HOSPITAL CARNIVAL 1939. The Fancy Dress. Amongst those taking part were: Victor Batts, Heather Burden, Clara Wright, Brenda Shadbolt, Sheila Miles, Bob Brindle, Robert Weston, Rita Burden, Mick Lewis.

WPC MRS PENTELOW & SGT. MUSTON 'On Duty' at the 1922 General Election.

THE YOUNGEST LADY STEEPLE-JACK IN ENGLAND
MISS OLIVE WAINWRIGHT AT THE TOP OF THE BLISS TWEED MILL CHIMNEY
— CHIPPING NORTON AUGUST 1919 —

THE FUNERAL OF THE LATE MRS MACE. The bearers were Mr John Shadbolt, Mr Alfred Pratt and Mr Margetts. Her husband Mr Thomas Mace who died in 1916 was Town Clerk for many years.

THE BAND OF HOPE PROCESSION on the way to their annual tea.

GIRL GUIDES and other organisations on parade in Horse Fair.

NATIONAL CHILDREN'S HOMES FÊTE in 1908.

NATIONAL CHILDREN'S HOMES FÊTE in 1923. Mr Weston and his helper Tom Heath running the Hoopla stall.

JIM SHADBOLT AND JACK BRAIN with Mrs Dodds-Parker 'bowling for the pig'. Onlookers include Kathleen Chapman, Mr Freddie Warmington, Miss S. Webb (Mayor), Mrs C. King (Mayoress) and Sister Little 1951.

VALENTINE DAY. An old custom peculiar to Chipping Norton. During the early hours the children of the town gathered in a group and walked round the streets chanting:

'Please to give us a Valentine,
I'll be yours if you'll be mine'.

The local shopkeepers would then throw out sweets or hot copper coins and the children would scramble on the ground for them. Unfortunately this old custom was not kept after the late 1950s.

SECTION FIVE

Schools

A SCHOOL GROUP in 1913.

BOYS SCHOOL Teacher: Mr Brazington. Back row: Norman Cox, Bert Tucker, Bert Reeves, Ken Carter, Den Lewis, Ernie Batts, Geo Burman. Second row: Bill Brown, Geo Pick, Bernard Balfour, Bob Swann, Bill Bufton, Benj. Padley, Bill Watts. Third row: Stan Franklin, Dick Gibbs, Norman Keen, Ken Padley, Cecil Watts, Charlie Barnes, Ron Butler, Fred Broad. Front row: Charlie Morse, Walter Pickett, Cecil Viner, –?–, Frank Perry.

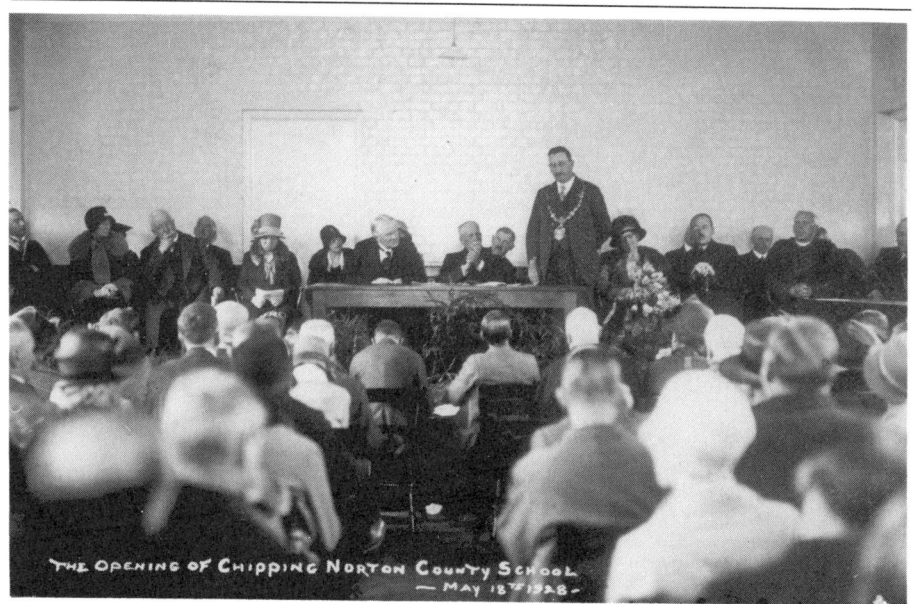

THE OPENING CEREMONY OF THE CHIPPING NORTON COUNTY SCHOOL with the Mayor, Mr Jack Marshall, 17 May 1928.

CHIPPING NORTON GRAMMAR SCHOOL.

THE CHURCH OF ENGLAND BOYS' SCHOOL in Church Street which is now the Vicarage.

THE BOYS CHURCH OF ENGLAND SCHOOL in May 1949. Headmaster: Mr Stanley Wykes. Back row: David Roberts, Peter Day, Brian Powers, Ken Berry, Terry Cox, Brian Allen, Ivor Howse, Alan Watkins. Middle row: Michael Goodman, Peter Watts, Bruce Durno, Syd Bailey, Peter Bridges, Tony Pick, Les Walton. Front row: John Grantham, David Clark, Paul Ashmore, Edward Price, Peter Johnston, Peter Clacy, Gilbert Clifton.

SECTION SIX

Winter

BRINGING THE MAIL up New Street from the station 1916. Mrs George Robinson and son Frank are standing in the porch of No. 25, now demolished for road widening.

SNOW IN CHURCH LANE.

THE KING'S HEAD YARD in 1931.

CHRISTMAS MORNING, 1925.

A SNOW SCENE in West Street.

THE 'GREAT SNOW' OF 1947. Snow drifts at Burford Corner.

SECTION SEVEN

Sport

CHIPPING NORTON GOLF CLUB, outside the Club House.

MRS HAMLETT (left) and partner teeing off.

SKATING on the common, 1929.

ICE HOCKEY on the lake, 1929.

HEYTHROP HUNT MEET at Boulters Barn, Churchill. On the left Albert Brassey, Master of the hunt from 1873 to 1918 and on the right is Charles Sturman, Huntsman from 1901 to 1922.

HEYTHROP HUNT KENNELS, Worcester Road, built in 1860.

CHIPPING NORTON TENNIS COURTS, Albion Street.

TENNIS MATCH, Chipping Norton vs. Hook Norton, 1923.

OVER NORTON ROAD TENNIS CLUB, 1914.

CRICKET MATCH, The town vs. Bliss Tweed Mill.

CHIPPING NORTON HOCKEY XI, 1927.

CHIPPING NORTON SWIFTS, 1906.

GEORGE HANNIS presenting the shield to Frank Miles (Captain).

CHIPPING NORTON FC. 1949–50 winners of OFA Benevolent Cup.

TUG-OF-WAR TEAM.

CHIPPING NORTON SPORTS CLUB – Hockey Section.

GRASS TRACK RACING AT CHIPPING NORTON. Cod Robinson is in second place.

BLEDINGTON RACES. From the left: Jimmy Smart, Ernie Morris, Charlie Simms and friends.

BASEBALL 'A' TEAM 1925 Back row left to right: Leo Berry, Horace Lowe, Chummy Gibbs, Horace Warmington, Alf Simms. Front row: Dennis Willetts, Gilbert Berry, Lance Hodgkins, Bernard King.

THE TOWN BASEBALL TEAM at an away match at Fairford, 9 September 1926.

BASEBALL TEAM OF THE FIFTIES. Seated, extreme right: Fred Lewis. Baseball was started in 1909 by Fred Lewis for a scout camp he was running, to rules credited to Arnold Doubleday of Coopertown, New York, USA who emigrated from Wootton near Woodstock. The Chipping Norton Baseball Club was founded in the 1920s. In 1926 a Chipping Norton team beat the London Americans at Stamford Bridge for the Championship of Great Britain.

At War

MEN OF THE OXFORDSHIRE REGIMENT on manœuvres in Chipping Norton.

WAR WORK — women threshing corn at Over Norton — September 1916.

THE SIXTEENTH LANCERS on army manœuvres in the town.

THE JAZZ BAND, peace celebrations in 1918.

A BONFIRE in the town centre to celebrate the Relief of Ladysmith.

RELIEF OF MAFEKING celebrations, 1901.

ASSEMBLING GAS MASKS at the Brewery.

WAR WEAPONS WEEK STALL in New Street. Left to right: Sheila Miles, Brenda Shadbolt, Clara Wright, Dawn Miles and Mrs Miles. Men unknown.

VJ TEA PARTY in Kings Head Yard, 15 August 1945.

ARMISTICE PARADE 1952. Front row: Bob Major, George Warmington, Mr Holmes (Town Clerk), Miss Sybil Webb (Major), Jack Marshall, Inspector Brooks, George Hughes (Mace Bearer), Sergeant Cato.

Entertainments

THE MYSTIC DANCE BAND: Jim Robinson, Bill Pick, Bill Townley, Elsie Luckett and Jack Brain.

TEDDY DIX and his dance band at the Norton Hall.

CIRCUS ELEPHANTS proceeding down New Street. The old gas office in the background was demolished when the cinema was built.

CIRCUS PROCESSION through the town.

THE NEW CINEMA IN NEW STREET. Now the squash courts.

OFFICIAL OPENING OF THE NEW STREET CINEMA in 1934. The mayor, Mr Swann, and his wife, with Sidney Hall on the right and Bob Major on the left.

CHIPPING NORTON SILVER BAND in the Town Hall.

THE BAND on the Town Hall steps.

WILFRED PICKLES 'Have A Go' live from Chipping Norton Town Hall, in the 1950s.

COBHAM'S FLYING DISPLAY Chipping Norton, 1933.

Organisations

CHIPPING NORTON BOY SCOUT PACK c. 1925 Back row: Frank Shepherd, Son Pratt, Den Lewis, Ernie Tanner, Charlie Morse. Third row: Arthur Stanley, Charlie Wilson, –?–, Miss Bunn, Fred Lewis, Officer from Church Army. Second row: Arthur Hess, Les Witts, George Rice, Bernard King, John Crook, Arthur Killeby, John Morse, Bob Burford. Front row: Bob Turner, Roy Burford, Percy Hunt, Alf Hess, Joe Townley, Bob Sewell, George Lamb, Fred Clacy.

CHIPPING NORTON PIONEER SCOUTS with their leader Fred Lewis. This pack was one of the first to be formed in the country in 1907.

AMONGST THE GUIDES ON THIS PICTURE, taken c. 1920, are Kath Lewis, Spud Taylor, Olive Simms, Mona Woodward, Phyllis Brooks, Hilda Hovard, Alice Burden, Kath Cole, Lily Warmington and May Ford.

CHIPPING NORTON GUIDES AND BROWNIES knitting squares for Mother Theresa, 1969.

THE OLD BALCONY in the Town Hall.

STOUR CHORAL UNION COMPETITION, 1924. Chipping Norton Baptist Children's Choir. Back row: Geo. Fiddes, Wilf Burson, Walter Sallos, Eileen Lewis, Ethel Biggerstaff, Gladys Roberts, — Goodman, Phyllis Swann, John Morse. Second row: Ray Swann, Joan Roberts, Dennis Lewis, Joyce Bailey, Bert Reeves, Ernie Batts, Benj Padley, Dulcie Packer, Ethel Burbidge. Third row: Ernie Withers, Muriel Meades, — Stanley, Cecil Watts, Bob Swann, Roy Worville, Ivy Worville, Eileen Meades. Front row: Gwyneth Burbidge, Ted Watts, Les Reeves, Ivy Webb, Charlie Morse, Fred Burbidge.

WOMENS' INSTITUTE CHRISTMAS PARTY, 1953.

OPENING OF THE BRITISH LEGION CLUB by Sir Ian Fraser MP on 19 February 1955. On the right of Sir Ian is Colonel Chamberlayne, Branch President and Mayor of Chipping Norton. On the left of Sir Ian is Dr Russell, Treasurer and next to him is Mr W. Hutchinson, Chairman.

The Fire Service and Transport

A FIRE ENGINE leaves the old engine house in Burford Road on its way to a fire at Dean.

OFF TO A FIRE AT BLEDINGTON. The steamer is being pulled by one of Hitchman's lorries.

TOWN HALL FIRE, 3 March 1950.

FIRE AT PRIESTLANDS SHOP Middle Row, 9 December 1950. Rebuilt and now called Market House Restaurant.

FIRE AT TARGET STABLES, Burford Road. Captain A.E. Mace on the left.

FIRE AT ENSTONE 1932, attended by Chipping Norton and Charlbury engines.

FIRE AT MR KEEN'S COTTAGE, Kingham.

CHIPPING NORTON STATION and the road leading to the Bliss Tweed Mill.

ENGINE WAITING OUTSIDE THE ENGINE SHED and, in the foreground, a wagon carrying the gas bottles which were used to fuel the lighting in railway carriages. The avenue of trees behind is the site of the old mill tramway.

THE LEYS looking from the Common over the railway goods yard. Five of the wagons shown belong to William Bliss.

ENGINE NO. 1473 *Fair Rosamund* photographed at Chipping Norton station with the staff and Wallace, the station cat.

THE LAST PASSENGER TRAIN from Chipping Norton to Kingham on 3 December 1962.

CHIPPING NORTON JUNCTION. The name of the station was changed to Kingham in May 1909.

KINGHAM STATION showing the old south signal box which was built against the road bridge and towered above it.

KINGHAM STATION.

HOOK NORTON STATION with the 'Port to Port' Express passing through.

HOOK NORTON VIADUCT.

MR BURDEN'S LORRY transporting Putmans marquee. The lorry driver is Mr M. Nurden.

MR WEBB with his new van.

THE WHITE HART BUS – used for conveying guests and their baggage to and from the station.

MOTORCYCLISTS outside the Victoria Restaurant, West Street (now Highlights).

HARTWELL AND BARLOW LTD, Horse Fair (now Central Tyre Co.).

MOTHERS' UNION ANNUAL OUTING.

YOUNG AND MAJORS GARAGE, London Road (where No. 2 London Road now stands).

YOUNG AND MAJORS subsequent garage at the bottom of London Road.

ACCIDENT IN NEW STREET. The Policeman with the walking stick (left) is Superintendent Cox.

BUCKLAND'S ROUNDABOUTS overturned in New Street while on their way to Stow Fair in 1904.

SECTION TWELVE

Villages

OVER NORTON HOUSE from the Park.

OVER NORTON WI Coronation Garden Party.

MAY DAY at Over Norton, 1923.

CHOICEHILL ROAD, Over Norton, showing the old shelter.

OVER NORTON VILLAGE, NEAR CHIPPING NORTON   55715

CENTRE OF OVER NORTON showing the large elm – later felled.

SPORTING YOUNG BRITAIN. The village team in training for future contests. The youth of Britain now get such athletic training at school that the contest is very keen in all kinds of sports. The youngsters on the home-made tryke set the pace down hill. Taken at Over Norton, Oxfordshire.
Photograph and caption from the National Press in the 1930s.

CHURCH STREET, Charlbury, looking towards the Bull Inn.

ANOTHER VIEW OF CHURCH STREET, Charlbury.

OLD VIEW OF CHARLBURY.

THE OLD TOLL HOUSE, Charlbury.

CHARLBURY TOWN CENTRE. The building behind the gas lamp is now the Tavern.

THE CORNER HOUSE AND THE BULL, Charlbury.

'FIVE WAYS', Charlbury.

STATION ROAD, Charlbury.

CHARLBURY AND DISTRICT FIRE BRIGADE ENGINE.

CHARLBURY STATION.

CHADLINGTON CORONATION DINNER.

CHADLINGTON. On the left is the butcher's shop and the building on the right is now Abbeyfield House.

CHADLINGTON HOUSE HOTEL, Chadlington.

THE NATIONAL CHILDREN'S HOME, Chadlington.

ENGLAND'S DRIEST SPOT. The Chequers Inn at Spelsbury burnt down on 24 September 1924.

MANOR FARM HOUSE, Spelsbury.

Heythrop House, near Chipping Norton

HEYTHROP HOUSE NEAR CHIPPING NORTON. Built by the Earl of Shrewsbury and gutted by fire in 1831. It was rebuilt by Thomas Brassey, the great railway builder, as a wedding present for his son, Albert Brassey, in 1870.

Heythrop Church.

HEYTHROP CHURCH.

Heythrop. - Roman Catholic and Priest's House (now demolished). Church

THE ROMAN CATHOLIC CHURCH at Heythrop built by Father Hefferman in 1826, near the mansion. It is now demolished.

Lidstone, Enstone 1904.

LIDSTONE, nr. Enstone in 1904.

THE HARROW, Enstone, showing the old cottage below the bridge.

ENSTONE CLUB DAY 1928.

PHOTO BY A. W. WHEELER.

HIGH STREET, HOOK NORTON.

PRODUCED BY B. R. MORLAND, BANBURY.

Sold by J. Spatcher, Hook Norton.

HIGH STREET, Hook Norton.

HOOK NORTON, looking towards the Nettings.

HOOK NORTON, with the school on the right.

GREAT TEW, showing the Falkland Arms and the stocks.

THE SCHOOL, Great Tew.

LITTLE TEW CHURCH.

VIEW OF GREAT ROLLRIGHT.

GREAT ROLLRIGHT RECTORY, now demolished.

RICHARD WITHERS. Born on 11 October 1805 at Burmington, near Shipston-on-Stour, Warwickshire, Richard spent most of his life as a shepherd. He lived at Potters Combes, a cottage near to St Andrews Church in Great Rollright. Before he died at the age of 104 in 1910, Richard smoked three ounces of tobacco a week.

BRUERN ABBEY. Built in the grounds near to where the Cistercian Abbey once stood.

SARSDEN HOUSE, burnt down in 1689, rebuilt in 1693 and altered and renovated by James Langston.

A TEAM OF HORSES returning home, passing the Old Stone Cross at Sarsden.

THE FOUNTAIN, Churchill, built in 1870 by the Earl of Ducie as a memorial to James Haughton Langston and his wife Julia Frances. It was formerly part of the village water supply.

CHURCHILL CHURCH, built by James Haughton Langston in 1826, the tower being two-thirds the size of Magdalen College tower, Oxford.

CHURCHILL FLOWER SHOW, 1923.

CHASTLETON HOUSE, built in 1614 by Walter Jones and never altered or added to.

CORNWELL VILLAGE before it was rebuilt, in the 1930s.

THE FOUR SHIRE STONE, where the counties of Oxford, Gloucester, Warwick and Worcester formerly met. In the 1930s the Worcestershire boundary was altered and now only three counties meet here.

FIFIELD CHURCH.

THE MERRYMOUTH INN, Fifield, thought to be named after the old village name of Merrymouth Fifield.

THE TOMB AT IDBURY, OF SIR BENJAMIN BAKER, designer of the Forth railway bridge.

LEAFIELD WIRELESS STATION, which commenced operating in 1922 with a major extension in 1966 and closed as a wireless station in 1986. It was used mostly for Reuter News Agency and Maritime Service.

THE CROSS HANDS INN, kept for many years by the Bartlett family.

SALFORD CHURCH.

SALFORD FÊTE, 1927.

A STREET VIEW of Milton-under-Wychwood.

A FIRE at Alfred Groves & Sons' builders yard, Milton-under-Wychwood in 1926.

SHIPTON COURT. The present Mansion was finished in 1603, probably on the site of an older house, by Rowland, afterwards Sir Rowland de Lacy. It was sold by his descendent to Sir Compton Reade, in 1663, in whose family it remained until 1868. It was left by the late Sir John Reade to Mr Joseph Wakefield, who took the name of Reade.

CHAPEL LANE, Shipton-under-Wychwood.

CHURCH AND SCHOOL AT KINGHAM. The school was pulled down in 1920.

EMPIRE DAY CELEBRATIONS, 1928.

A VIEW OF KINGHAM VILLAGE.

THE ROLLRIGHT STONES. The Rollright Stones are a ceremonial stone circle probably dating from c. 2500–2000 BC. Nearby are the Whispering Knights, five stones, possibly part of a burial chamber. A few yards away, in Warwickshire, stands a lone stone eight feet high called the King Stone. A famous legend tells that all these stones were originally a king and his men who were turned into stone by a witch.

ROLL RIGHT STONES THE KING STONE. 10.

ACKNOWLEDGEMENTS

Acknowledgements for use of photographs from the following members of the Chipping Norton Local History Society:
Alan Brain, Keith Cooper-Harris, Eileen Forbes, Edward Jones, Muriel Keene, Dennis Lewis, Brenda Morris, Peter Tyrrell, Pauline Watkins, Alan Watkins.